Nan and Lad

by Tristan Horrom
illustrated by Anni Matsick

Decodable 3

I0806522

McGraw Hill Education

Bothell, WA • Chicago, IL • Columbus, OH • New York, NY

MHEonline.com

Send all inquiries to:
McGraw-Hill Education
8787 Orion Place
Columbus, OH 43240

ISBN: 978-0-02-138943-8
MHID: 0-02-138943-8

Printed in China

9 10 11 12 13 DSS 28 27 26 25 24

I have Nan.

I have Lad.

Nan naps.
Lad laps.

Nan and Lad land.

Damp as Nan!

Damp as Lad!